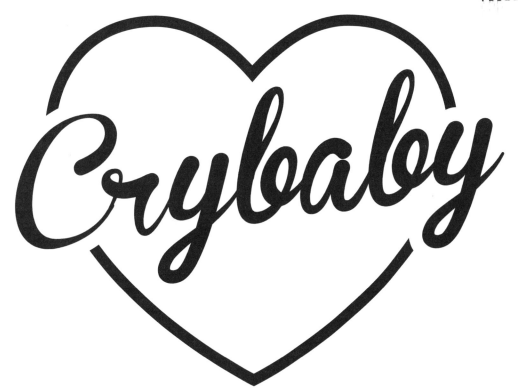

CONCEIVED BY
Melanie Martinez

ARTWORK BY
Chloe Tersigni

Published by:
ULYSSES PRESS
P.O. Box 3440
Berkeley, CA 94703
www.ulyssespress.com

ISBN: 978-1-61243-686-9

Printed in Canada by Marquis Book Printing

16 18 20 19 17 15

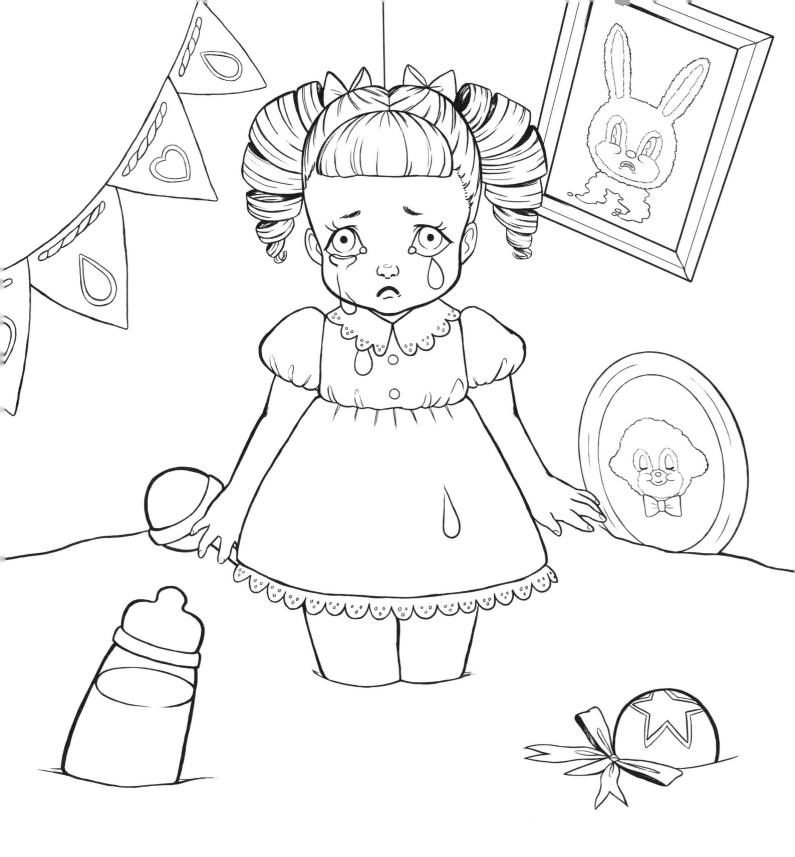

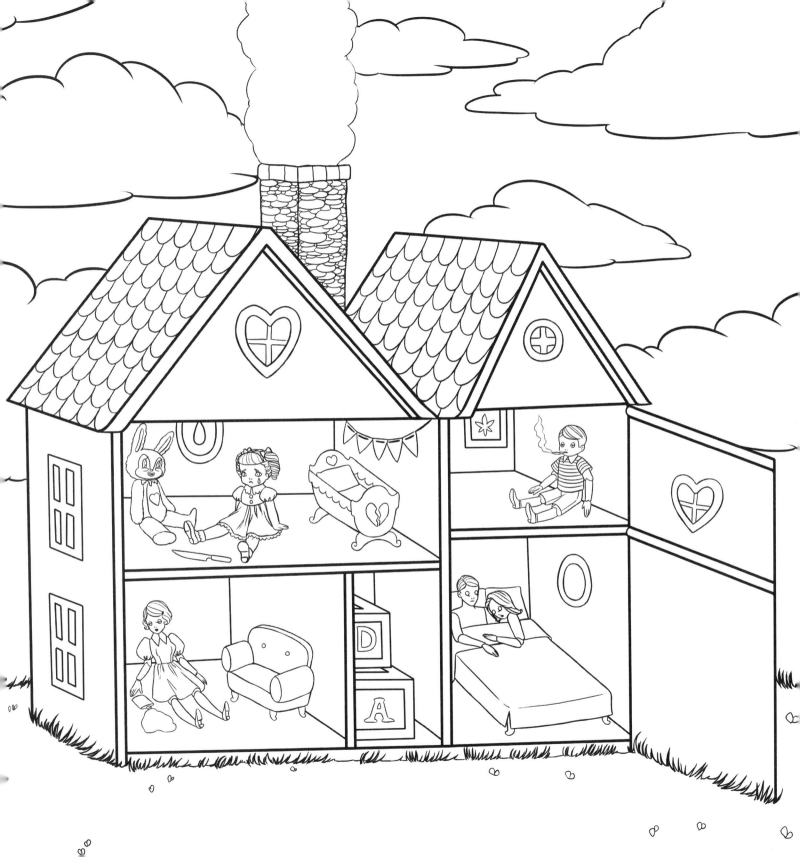

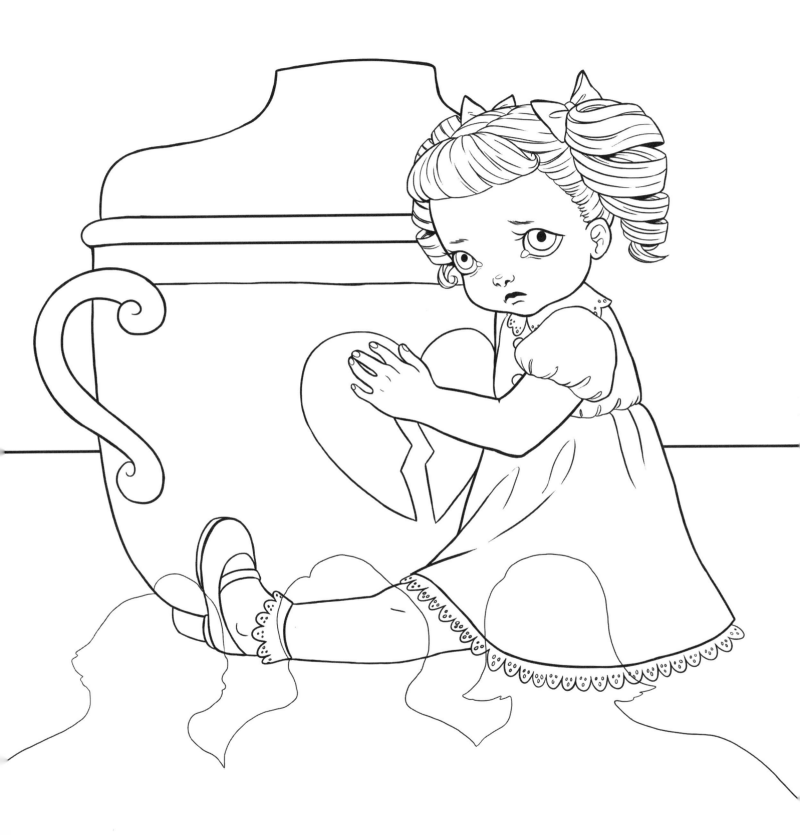

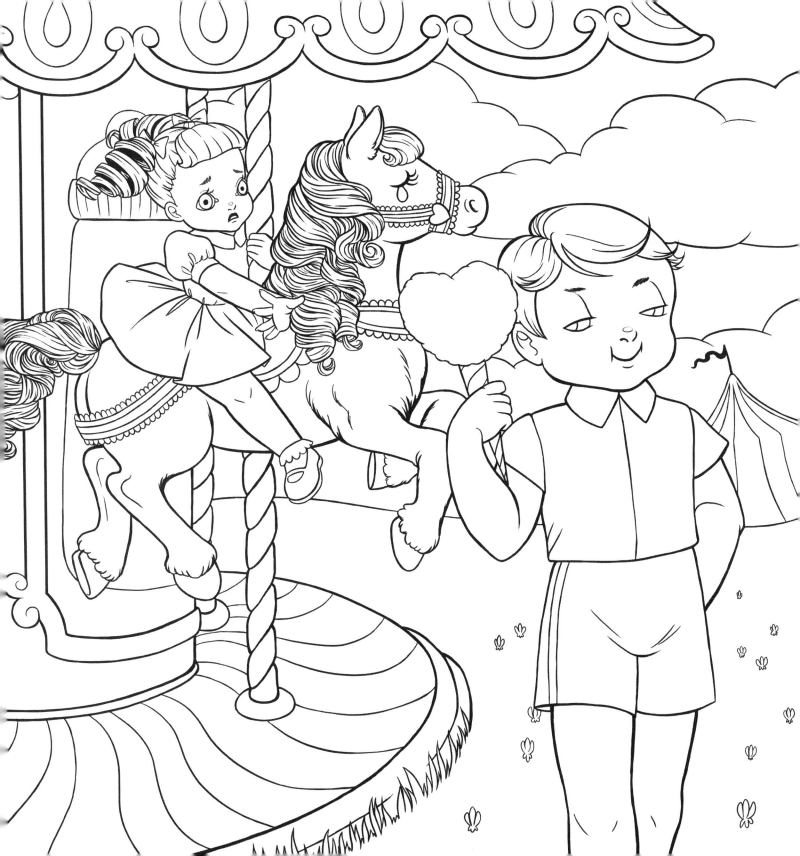

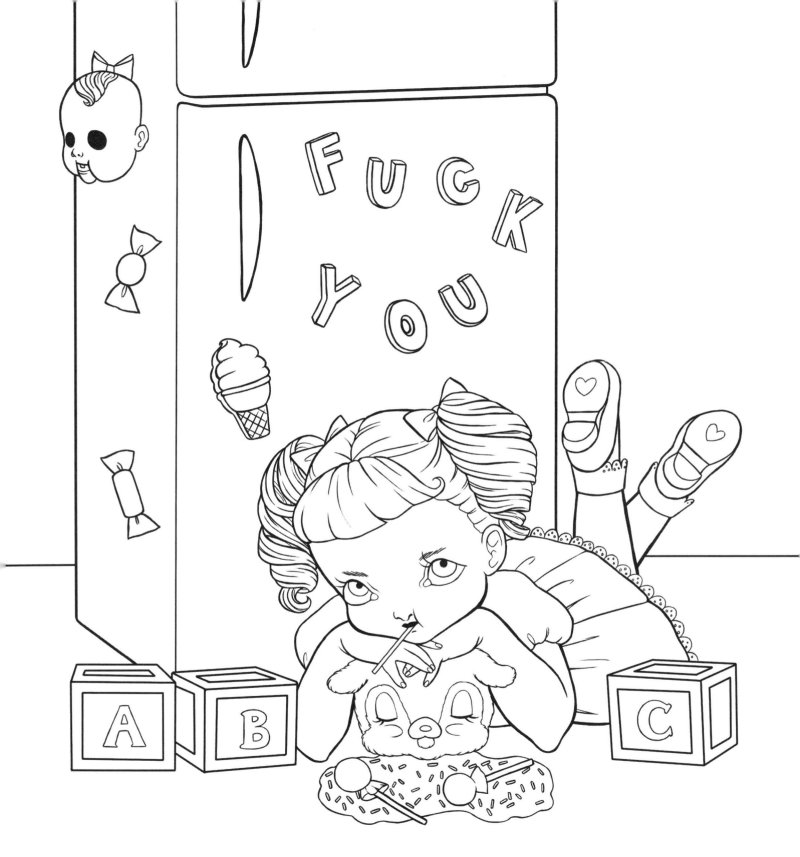

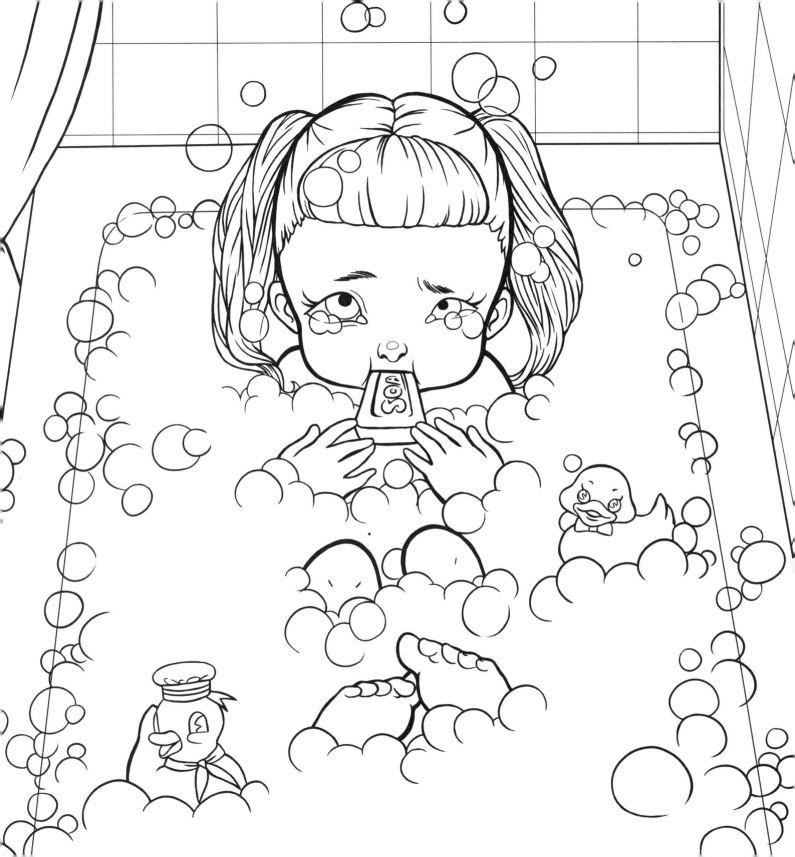

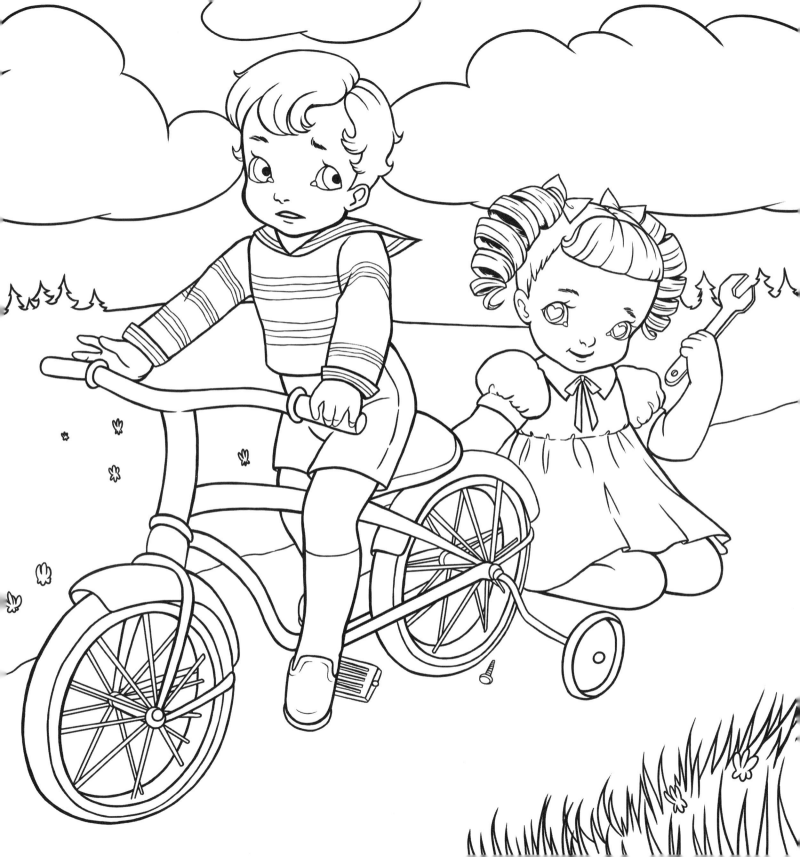

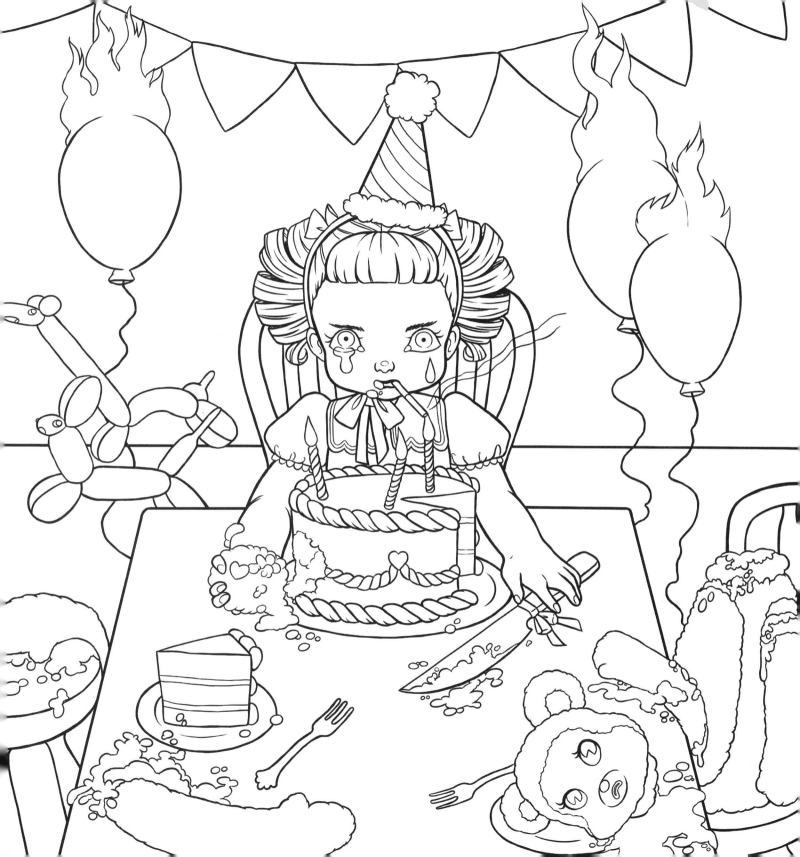

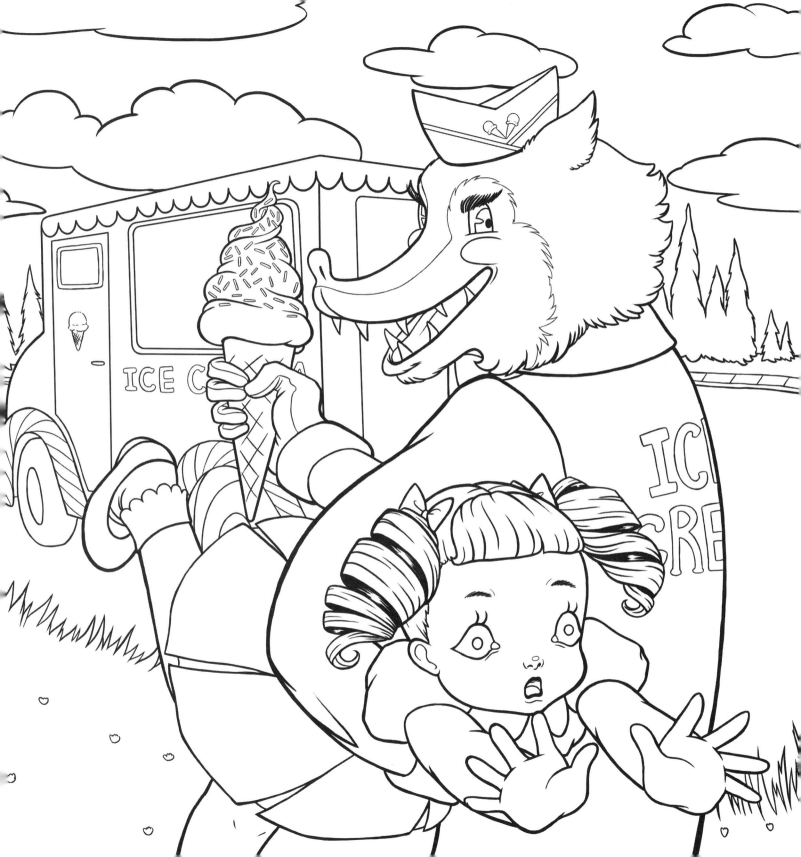

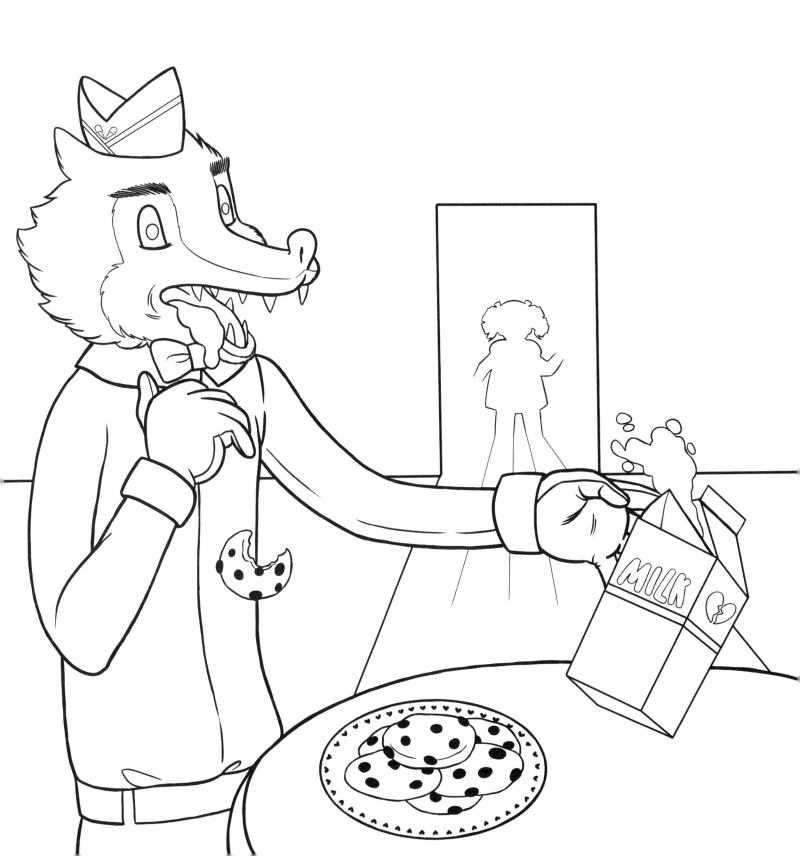

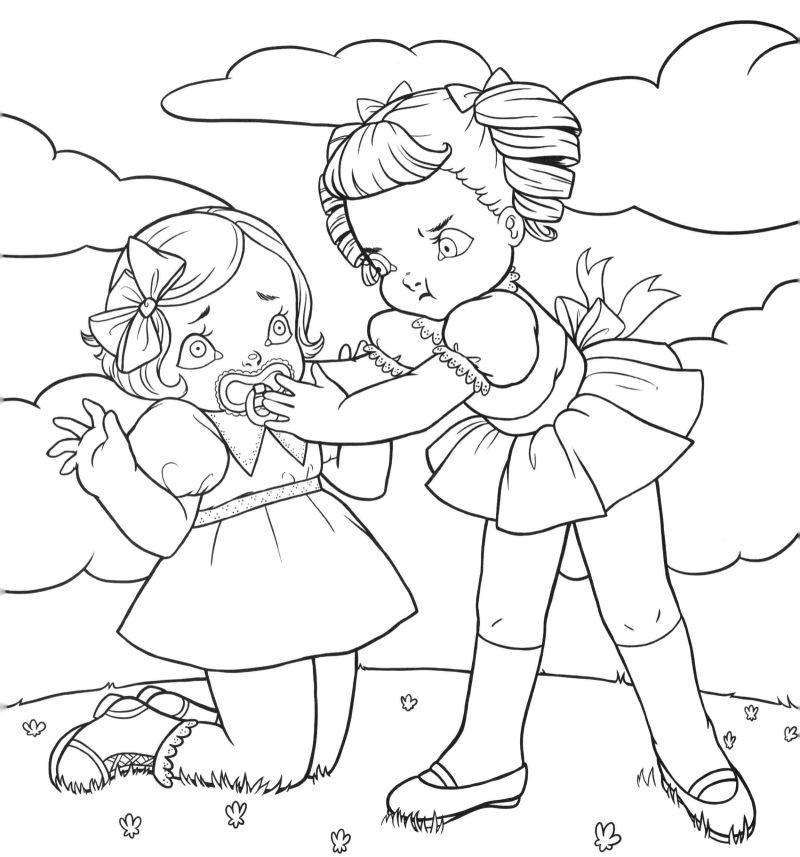

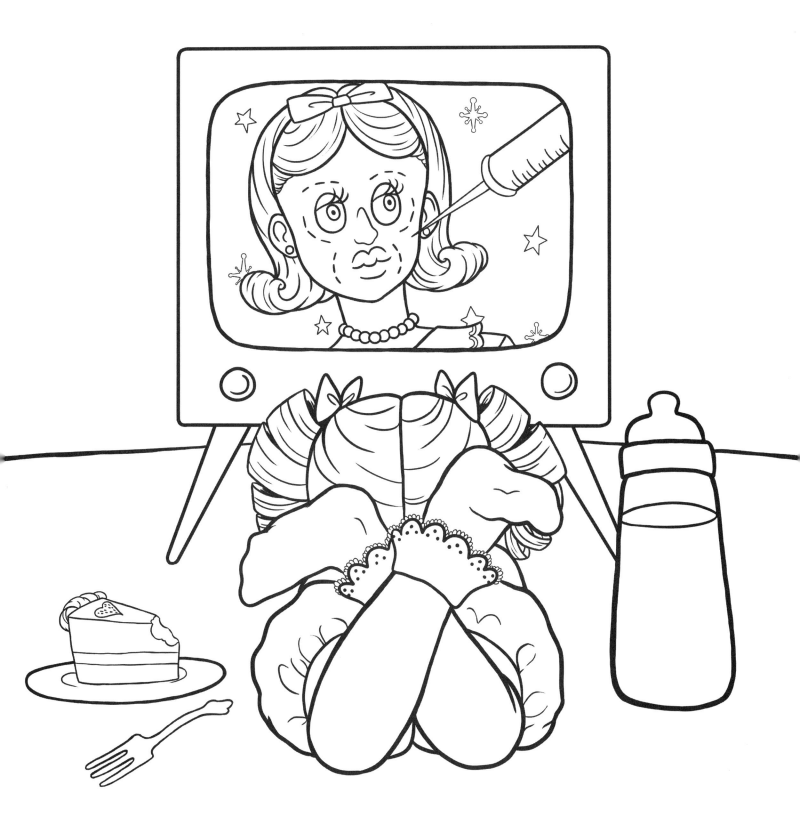

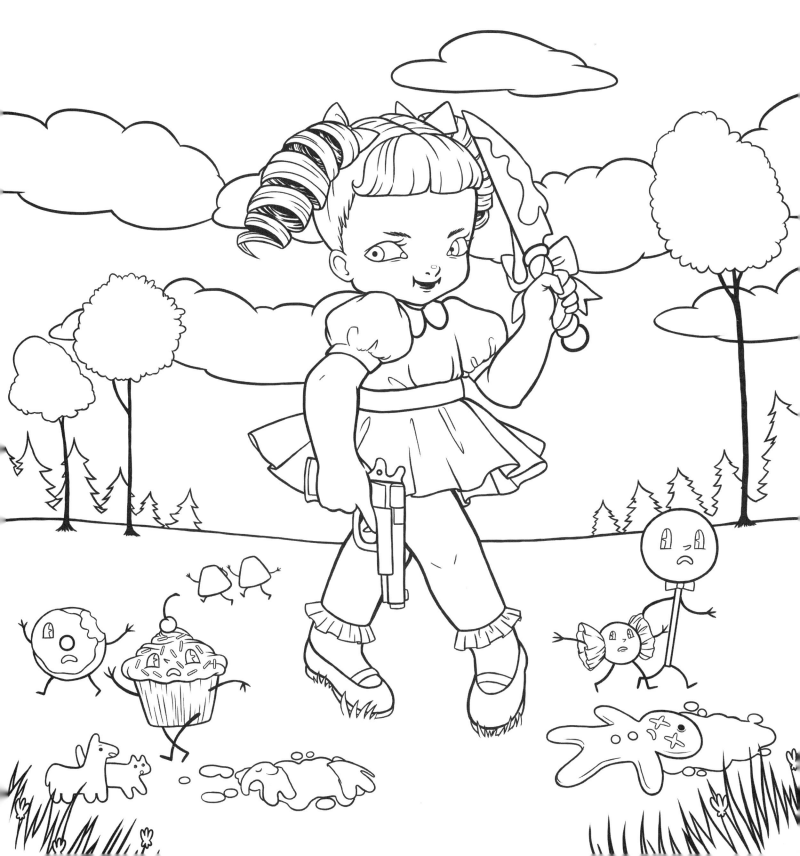

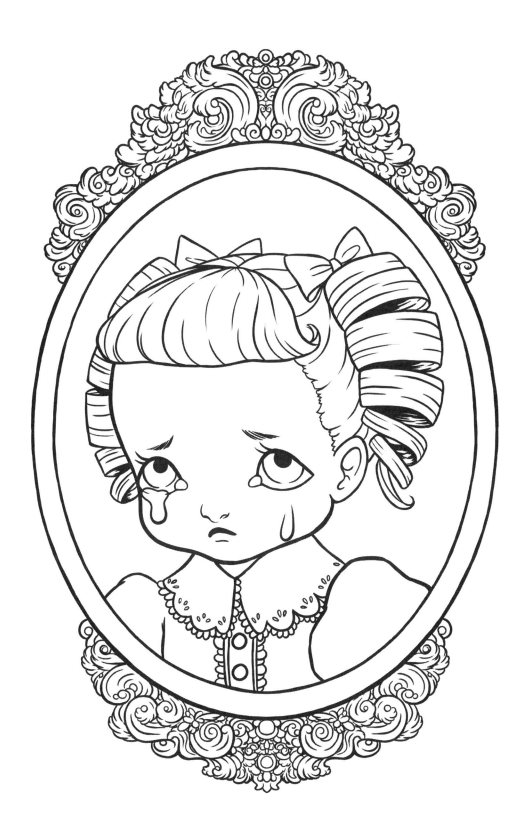

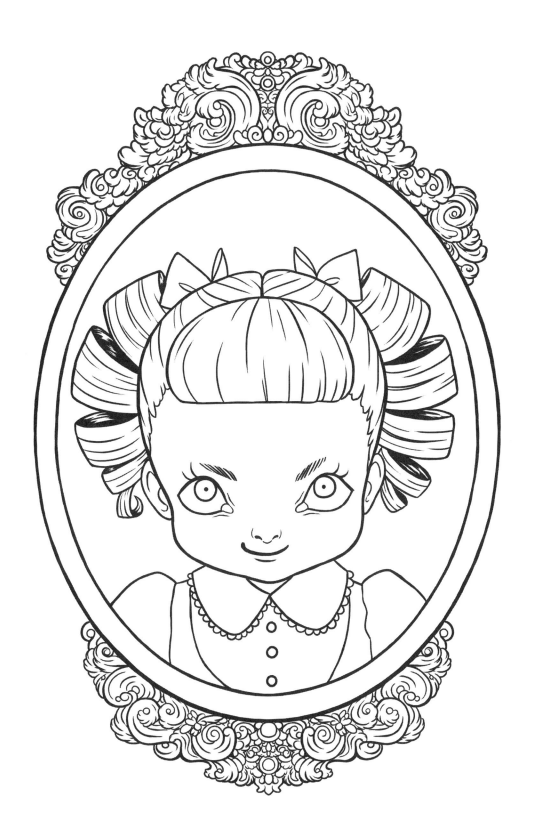

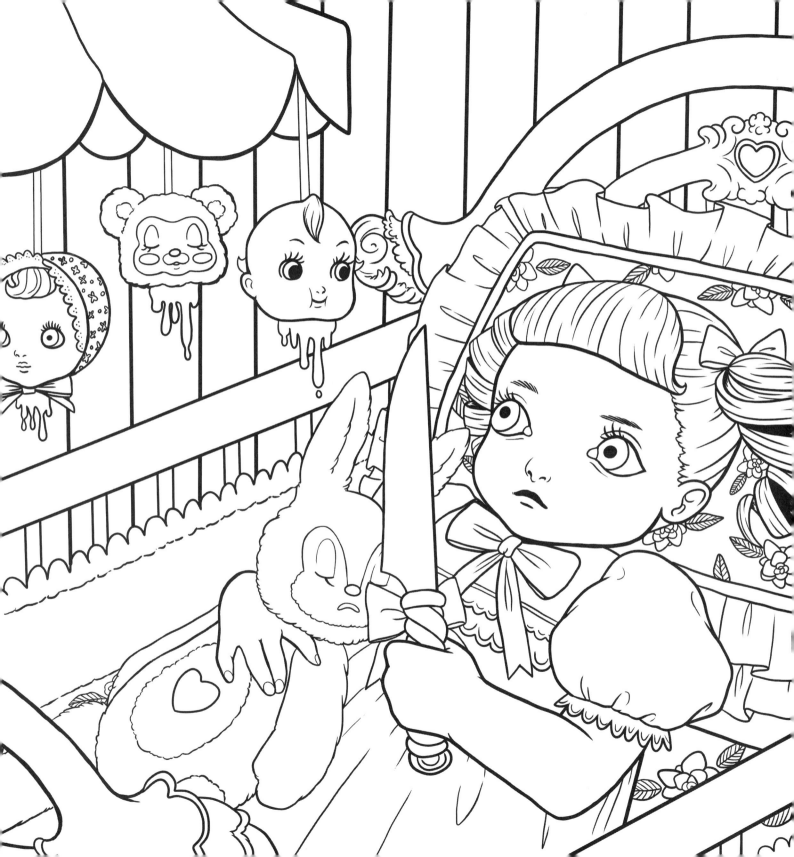

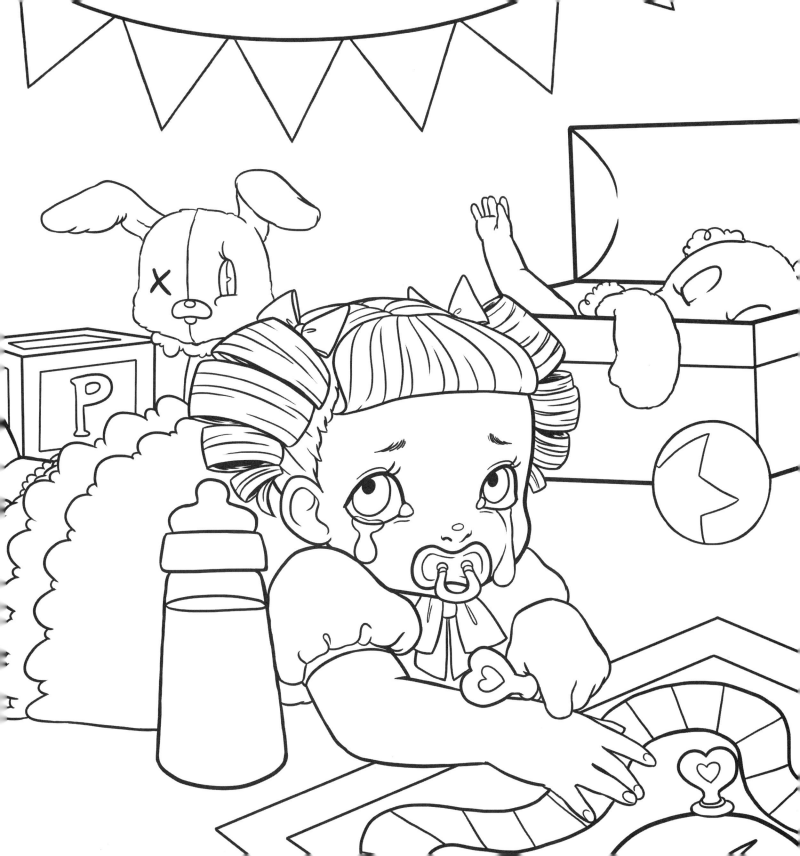

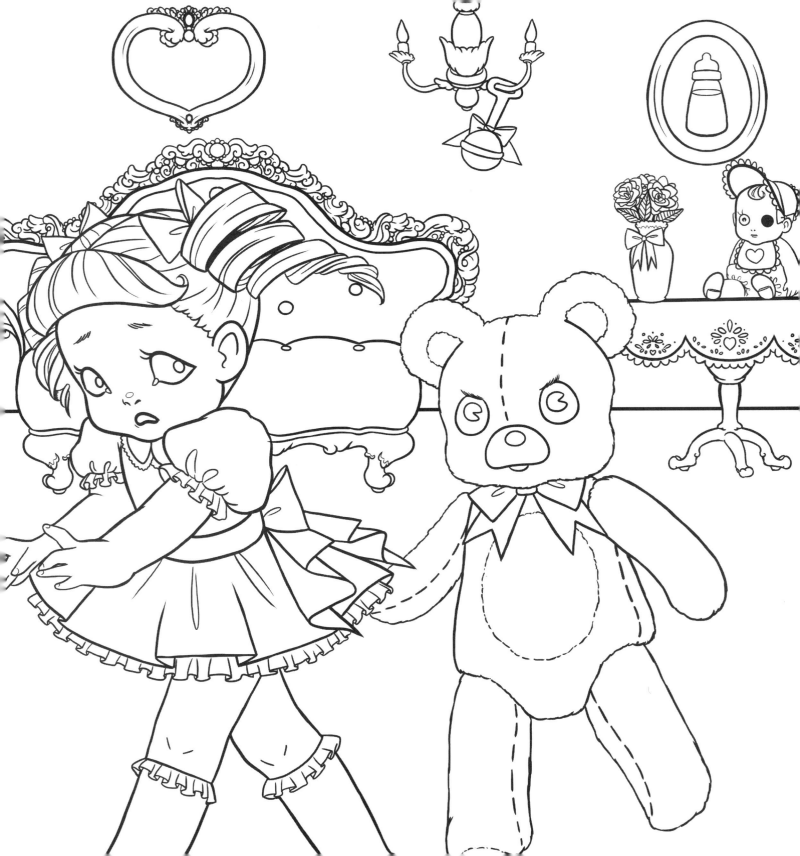

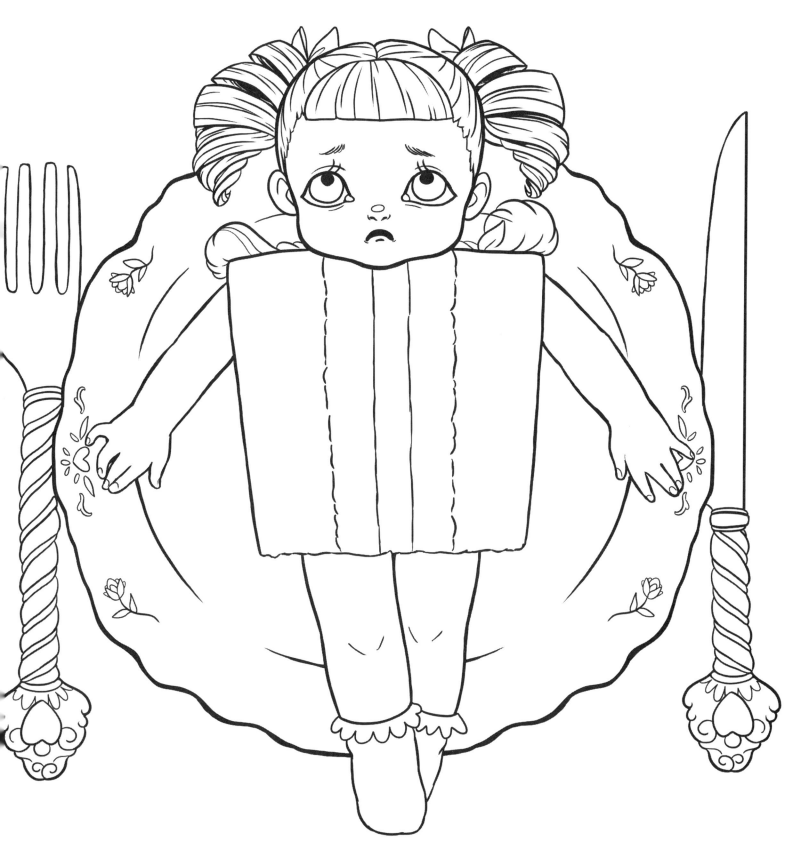